MAP BASICS

TYPES of MAPS

CANADA
Hudson Bay
BRITISH COLUMBIA
ALBERTA
SASKATCHEWAN
MANITOBA
ONTARIO
QUÉBEC
NEWFOUNDLAND
UNITED STATES
WASHINGTON
OREGON
CALIFORNIA
NEVADA
IDAHO
MONTANA
WYOMING
UTAH
ARIZONA
COLORADO
NEW MEXICO
NORTH DAKOTA
SOUTH DAKOTA
NEBRASKA
KANSAS
OKLAHOMA
TEXAS
MINNESOTA
IOWA
MISSOURI
ARKANSAS
LOUISIANA
WISCONSIN
MICHIGAN
OHIO
KENTUCKY
TENNESSEE
MISSISSIPPI
ALABAMA
GEORGIA
FLORIDA
VIRGINIA
NEW YORK
NEW YORK CITY
PHILADELPHIA
CHICAGO
LOS ANGELES
Gulf of Mexico
CUBA

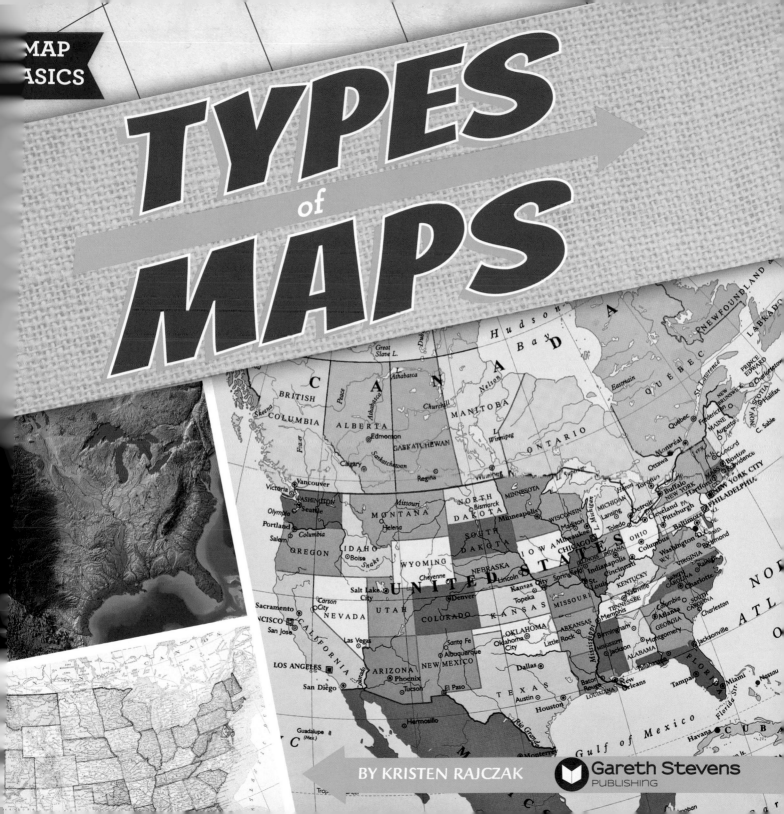

BY KRISTEN RAJCZAK

Gareth Stevens PUBLISHING

Please visit our website, www.garethstevens.com. For a free color catalog of all our high-quality books, call toll free 1-800-542-2595 or fax 1-877-542-2596.

Library of Congress Cataloging-in-Publication Data

Rajczak, Kristen.
Types of maps / by Kristen Rajczak.
p. cm. — (Map basics)
Includes index.
ISBN 978-1-4824-1064-8 (pbk.)
ISBN 978-1-4824-1065-5 (6-pack)
ISBN 978-1-4824-1063-1 (library binding)
1. Maps — Juvenile literature. I. Rajczak, Kristen. II. Title.
GA105.6 R35 2015
526—d23

First Edition

Published in 2015 by
Gareth Stevens Publishing
111 East 14th Street, Suite 349
New York, NY 10003

Designer: Sarah Liddell
Editor: Kristen Rajczak

Photo credits: Cover, pp. 1 (upper left map), 13 AridOcean/Shutterstock.com; cover, p. 1 (lower left) Jim Pruitt/Shutterstock.com; cover, p. 1 (right) iStock/Thinkstock.com; p. 5 Noel Hendrickson/Photodisc/Thinkstock.com; p. 7 DEA/A. DAGLI ORTI/De Agostini/Getty Images; p. 9 (main) Encyclopaedia Britannica/Universal Images Group/Getty Images; p. 9 (compass rose) Zmiter/Shutterstock.com; pp. 11, 19, 21 ekler/Shutterstock.com; p. 15 Globe Turner/Shutterstock.com; p. 17 Agrus/Shutterstock.com.

Printed in the United States of America

CPSIA compliance information: Batch #CS15GS: For further information contact Gareth Stevens, New York, New York at 1-800-542-2595.

CONTENTS

Words in the glossary appear in **bold** type the first time they are used in the text.

USE A MAP

Do you want to visit a friend in a different city? You can use a map to plan your route. Would you like to know what the landscape of a certain park is like? Another kind of map can help you with that!

Maps are pictures that **represent** the surface of Earth. They're tools that can show distance, direction, and the size and shape of the land. Maps often give **information** about the areas they show, such as how many people live there.

JUST THE FACTS

Most maps are flat, or two-dimensional.

CANADA
ONTARIO
Nutrition Facts
Valeur nutritive

Though there are many types of maps, the basics of reading them are the same.

MAP HISTORY

The earliest proof of mapmaking dates back to about 2300 BC! Babylonians who lived in present-day Iraq and near the Persian Gulf used clay tablets to draw maps. However, many people think even earlier civilizations made maps, too.

During the 2nd century AD, a Greek named Ptolemy put together a map of the world based on his studies of **geography** and math. Ptolemy's work was rediscovered around 1300. Cartographers of the time used it as a starting point for future maps and exploration.

JUST THE FACTS

Someone who makes maps is called a cartographer. Making maps is called cartography.

FAVO
NIVS
CHORVS
OCCIDENS
CYRCI
NVS
ORIENS
SVBSOLANVS
BOREAS
SEPTEN
TRIO
ARABIA
FELIX
INDIA
EXTRA
GANGETI
CVS SI.
TAPRO
BANA IN.
LIBYA
AFRI
CA
EVRVS
VVLTVRNVS
AFRICVS
EVRONOTVS
LIBO
NOTVS
AVSTER
NOTOS
MERIDIES

This is a map from 1511 based on Ptolemy's work.

PARTS OF A MAP

Maps we use today commonly have a title, which tells what the map shows or is about. There's often a compass rose, too. It shows direction, including the cardinal directions of north, south, east, and west.

A map key, or legend, tells what **symbols** on the map mean. It may show what different colors stand for. Since maps are smaller than the area they represent, they have to be drawn using a scale, which is often listed on the map.

JUST THE FACTS

Because Earth is round and most maps are flat, maps cannot be totally ***accurate****. Some parts will be too big and others too small.*

A map scale lists what a small measurement on a map equals in distance on Earth. This map scale shows that every 1 1/8 inch (2.85 cm) equals 40 miles (64.4 km).

89°
INDIANA
88°
OHIO
TENNESSEE
Smithland
Princeton
Paducah
Eddyville
Wickliffe
Bardwell
Benton
Cadiz
Mayfield
Clinton
Murray
Hickman
Burlington
Covington
Alexandria
Independence
Warsaw
Brooksville
Falmouth
Carrollton
Wiliamstown
Maysville
Greenup
Bedford
Owenton
Mount Olivet
Vanceburg
Cynthiana
New Castle
La Grange
Flemingsburg
Carlisle
Grayson
Louisville
Frankfort
Georgetown
Owingsville
Morehead
Shelbyville
Paris
Versailles
Lexington
Mount Sterling
Sandy Hook
Taylorsville
Winchester
West Liberty
Brandenburg
Shepherdsville
Lawrenceburg
Frenchburg
Paintsville
Hawesville
Nicholasville
Stanton
Campton
Henderson
Hardinsburg
Bardstown
Uniontown
Owensboro
Harrodsburg
Irvine
Salyersville
Morganfield
Richmond
Elizabethtown
Springfield
Danville
Lancaster
Jackson
Hodgenville
Lebanon
Beattyville
Dixon
Calhoun
Leitchfield
Stanford
Booneville
Madisonville
McKee
Hartford
Campbellsville
Liberty
Mount Vernon
Hindman
Munfordville
Hazard
Greenville
Greensburg
London
White
Manchester
Hyden
Princeton
Brownsville
Somerset
Morgantown
Glasgow
Columbia
Russell Springs
Cumberland
Bowling Green
Edmonton
Hopkinsville
Barbourvillle
Harlan
Cadiz
Russellville
Scottsville
Burkesville
Monticello
Pineville
Elkton
Tompkinsville
Whitley City
Franklin
Albany
Williamsburg
Middlesboro
ntinuation of map,
set above.
map key
title
CITIES IN KENTUCKY
symbols
CITIES
State capitals
County seats
Cities
BOUNDARIES
State
County
map scale
0 20 40 mi
0 30 60 km
compass rose
N
E
S
W

POLITICAL MAPS

One of the most common types of map is a political map. A political map shows borders between countries and states. It can give lots of information or be very simple. A political map may have cities and capitals marked on it. Cities are often represented by a dot and capital cities by a star.

Look at the political map of Europe on the next page. It uses different colors and thin gray lines to show where one country ends and another starts.

JUST THE FACTS

A population map shows how many people live in an area. Often it's based on a political map. See some examples on page 21.

ICELAND
WHITE SEA
Arctic Circle
NORTH ATLANTIC OCEAN
SWEDEN
FINLAND
GULF OF BOTHNIA
NORWAY
ESTONIA
RUSSIA
LATVIA
BALTIC SEA
NORTH SEA
DENMARK
LITHUANIA
IRELAND
BELARUS
UNITED KINGDOM
POLAND
CELTIC SEA
NETHERLANDS
UKRAINE
GERMANY
BELGIUM
CZECH REPUBLIC
SLOVAKIA
LUX.
MOLDOVA
FRANCE
AUSTRIA
HUNGARY
BAY OF BISCAY
SWITZERLAND
ROMANIA
CROATIA
SLOVENIA
SERBIA
BOSNIA AND HERZEGOVINA
BLACK SEA
BULGARIA
LIGURIAN SEA
KOS.
RTUGAL
SPAIN
ITALY
ADRIATIC SEA
MONT.
MACE.
ALB.
AEGEAN SEA
GREECE
IONIAN SEA
MEDITERRANEAN SEA

This map only includes the names of countries. It also shows major bodies of water in light blue.

PHYSICAL MAPS

A physical map shows the geographic features of an area. Mountains, rivers, and lakes are often parts of the landscape included on physical maps. The colors used on the map show **relief**. Brown often represents higher **elevations**, and green shows plains. Water is most often shown in blue.

A topographic map is similar to a physical map. It uses contours, or specially curved lines that represent a certain height, to show the shape and elevation of an area.

JUST THE FACTS

When spaced closer together, contours show steepness. When farther apart, they show flatter parts of the landscape.

A physical map of North America shows the mountainous areas in shades of brown and the flatter parts in greens.

STREET VIEW

It used to be common for people to use maps to find their way when traveling. Road maps can still help you today, though. They show highways and where streets meet.

Road maps can show the whole United States, but they can also be of smaller areas. This allows for more **detail**, which can be helpful when you're in an unfamiliar city. Road maps often have landmarks and buildings on them, making them great tools for sightseeing, too.

JUST THE FACTS

*A set of numbers called coordinates can be used to direct someone to a place on a map. Coordinates are made up of measurements of the lines of **latitude** and **longitude** sometimes found on maps.*

PHOENIX, ARIZONA

PARK LANDMARK HOSPITAL INTERSTATE

0 0.5 1 mi
0 1 1.5 km

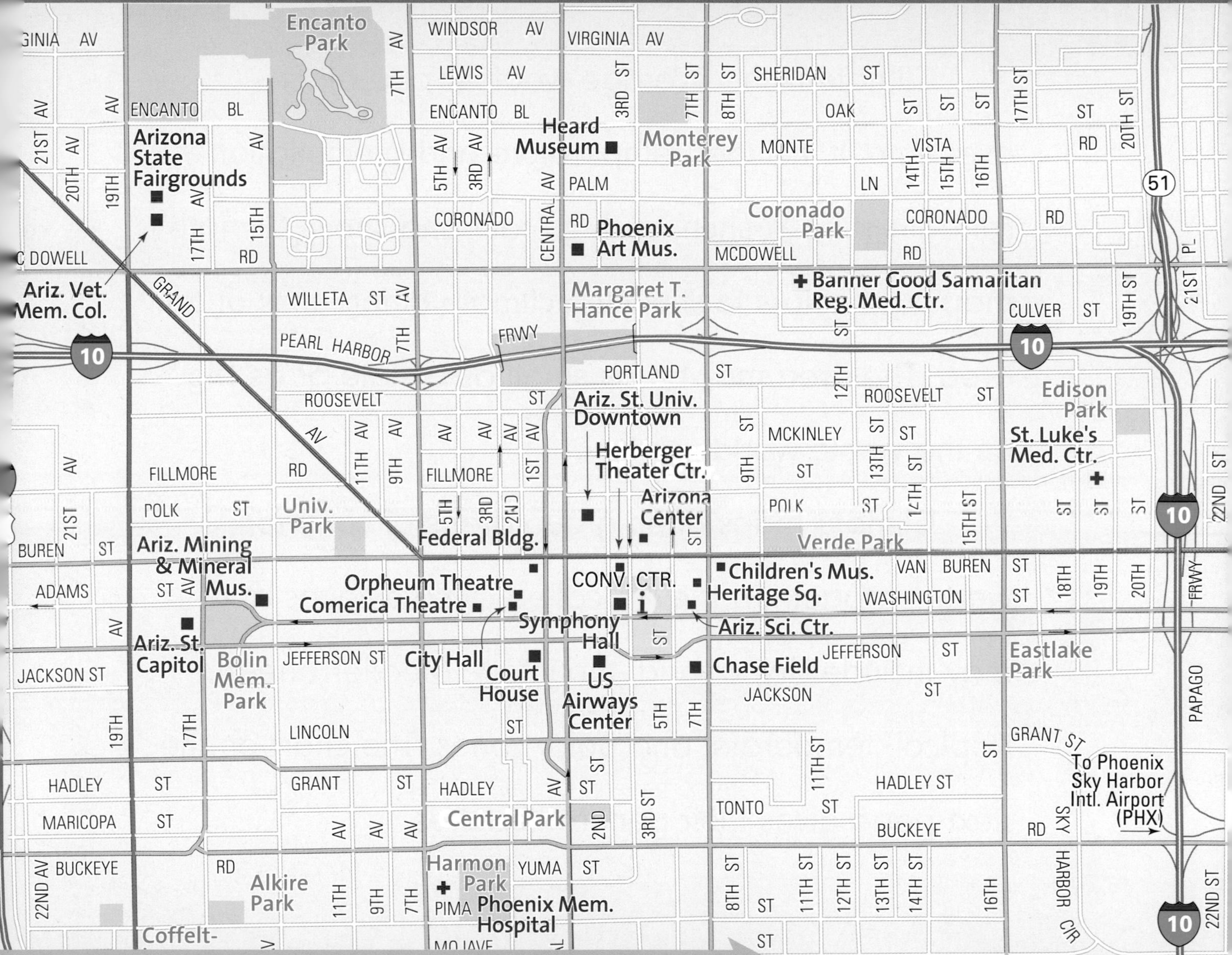

Encanto Park
Arizona State Fairgrounds
Ariz. Vet. Mem. Col.
Heard Museum
Monterey Park
Phoenix Art Mus.
Coronado Park
Banner Good Samaritan Reg. Med. Ctr.
Margaret T. Hance Park
Edison Park
St. Luke's Med. Ctr.
Ariz. St. Univ. Downtown
Herberger Theater Ctr.
Arizona Center
Univ. Park
Federal Bldg.
Verde Park
Ariz. Mining & Mineral Mus.
Orpheum Theatre
Comerica Theatre
CONV. CTR.
Children's Mus.
Heritage Sq.
Symphony Hall
Ariz. Sci. Ctr.
Ariz. St. Capitol
Bolin Mem. Park
City Hall
Court House
US Airways Center
Chase Field
Eastlake Park
To Phoenix Sky Harbor Intl. Airport (PHX)
Central Park
Harmon Park
Phoenix Mem. Hospital
Alkire Park
Coffelt-
Barrios Unidos Park
WINDSOR AV
VIRGINIA AV
LEWIS AV
SHERIDAN ST
ENCANTO BL
OAK
MONTE
VISTA
PALM
CORONADO RD
MCDOWELL RD
WILLETA ST
PEARL HARBOR FRWY
CULVER ST
PORTLAND ST
ROOSEVELT ST
MCKINLEY ST
FILLMORE RD
POLK ST
BUREN ST
VAN BUREN
ADAMS
WASHINGTON
JEFFERSON ST
JACKSON ST
LINCOLN
GRANT ST
HADLEY ST
MARICOPA ST
TONTO ST
BUCKEYE RD
YUMA ST
PIMA
MOJAVE
DURANGO AV
FREEWAY
GRAND AV
CENTRAL AV
PAPAGO FRWY
SKY HARBOR CIR
10
17
51

Don't have a **GPS**? No problem! Use a road map like this one to plan your route.

CHECKING OUT THE CLIMATE

Climate is the average weather of a place over time. It includes temperature and precipitation (prih-sih-puh-TAY-shun) such as rain and snow. Climate maps use colors to show the climate differences of an area. The area may be as small as a state or as big as the whole world!

Climate maps often group areas of common weather together. They're called climate zones and may include dry, or arid; mountain; Mediterranean; tropical; temperate; and polar zones. The chart on the next page gives their general features.

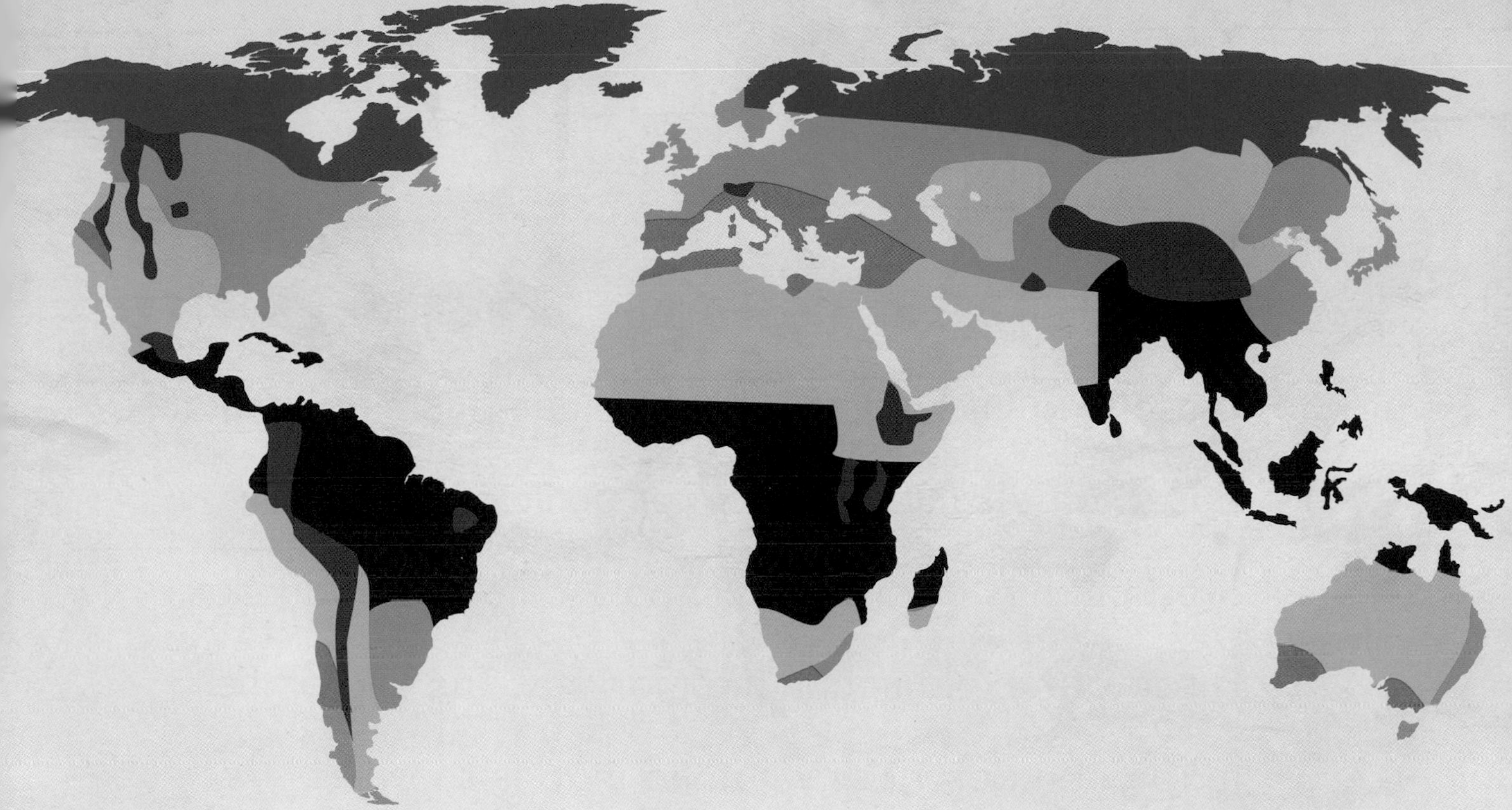

ZONE	FEATURES
arid	dry; temperature can vary greatly
mountain	cooler temperatures and more precipitation than the climate zone around it
Mediterranean	hot, dry summers and mild winters; cooler temperatures farther inland
polar	cold; dry
temperate	four seasons with warm summers and cold winters
tropical	hot; can be humid or dry

These climate zones are based on the work of German scientist Wladimir Köppen.

WHAT'S THE THEME?

A thematic map has a topic, or theme, it's presenting information about. A thematic map is often based on a simple physical or political map of an area but has additional symbols, colors, or markings. These are explained in the map key. The title of the map often describes what the map is showing.

A map of the world's **time zones** is one example of a thematic map. Maps of the United States showing election results by political party are another.

JUST THE FACTS

An economic map shows the economic activities, businesses, or natural resources of a place through symbols or colors. For example, a tiny bolt of lightning might represent a power plant.

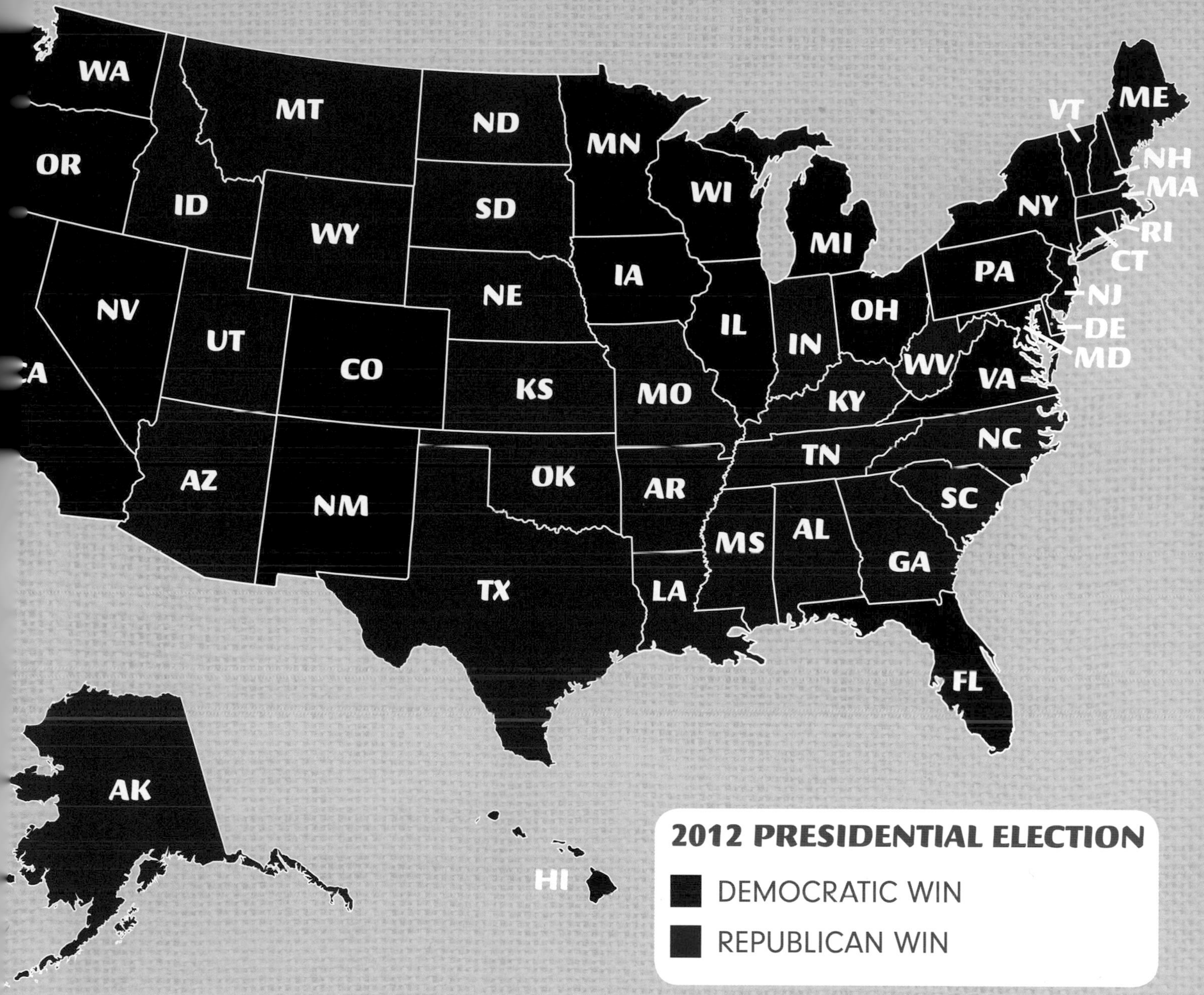
WA
MT
ND
MN
VT
ME
OR
NH
MA
ID
SD
WI
NY
WY
MI
RI
IA
PA
CT
NE
NJ
NV
OH
IL
DE
UT
IN
MD
WV
CO
VA
KS
MO
KY
NC
TN
OK
AZ
AR
SC
NM
AL
MS
GA
TX
LA
FL
AK
HI
2012 PRESIDENTIAL ELECTION
DEMOCRATIC WIN
REPUBLICAN WIN

On thematic maps of the United States showing election results, the Democratic political party is shown in blue. The Republican political party is shown in red.

THE GLOBE

Did you know globes are maps, too? Globes are round, like Earth, and so they can be more accurate than other maps. They often display the same detailed information as maps, but it's easier to understand the distance between places when looking at a globe. However, flat maps are much easier to carry around!

Now that you know many different types of maps, you can use them to learn about places around the world. Where do you want to go?

JUST THE FACTS

Cartographers make celestial maps, too. These are maps of stars, planets, and other heavenly bodies.

US POPULATION CHANGES

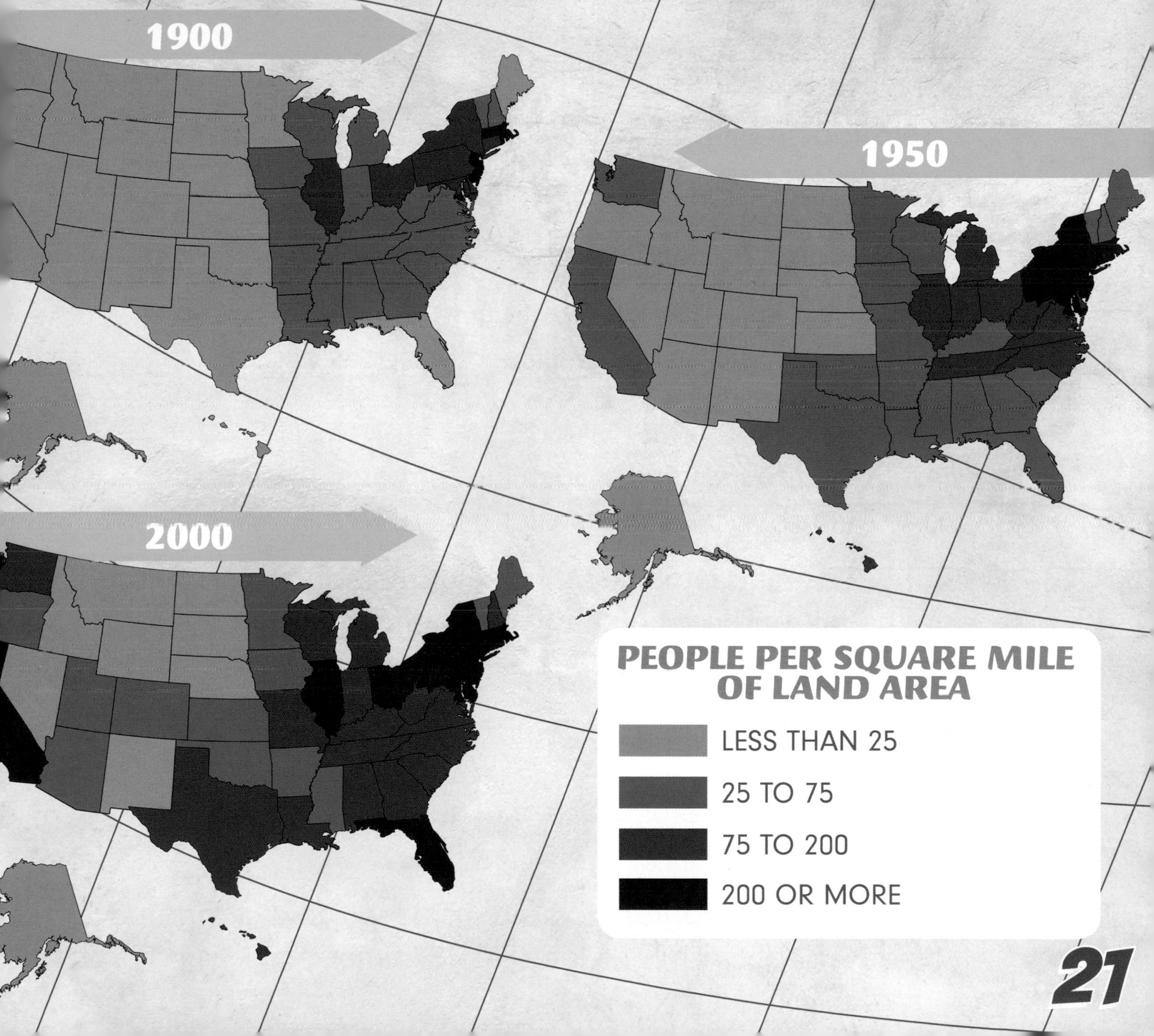

1900
1950
2000
PEOPLE PER SQUARE MILE OF LAND AREA
LESS THAN 25
25 TO 75
75 TO 200
200 OR MORE

GLOSSARY

accurate: free from mistakes

detail: a small part, or having to do with small parts

elevation: height above sea level

geography: the study of Earth

GPS: stands for Global Positioning System, a system that uses satellite signals to locate places on Earth

information: facts

latitude: the imaginary lines that run east and west above and below the equator

longitude: the imaginary lines that run north and south to the left and right of the Prime Meridian

relief: elevations of the land

represent: to stand for

symbol: a picture or shape that stands for something else

time zone: a geographic area inside which a standard time is used. Earth is divided into 24 time zones.

FOR MORE INFORMATION

BOOKS

Boswell, Kelly. *Maps, Maps, Maps!* North Mankato, MN: Capstone Press, 2014.

Waldron, Melanie. *Types of Maps.* Chicago, IL: Capstone Raintree, 2013.

WEBSITES

Maps: Adventure Island
education.nationalgeographic.com/education/multimedia/interactive/maps-tools-adventure-island/kd/?ar_a=3
Learn more about maps by playing this game from National Geographic.

Reading a Map
www.nps.gov/webrangers/activities/readingmap/?id=21
Check out this interactive website about map reading from the National Park Service.

Publisher's note to educators and parents: Our editors have carefully reviewed these websites to ensure that they are suitable for students. Many websites change frequently, however, and we cannot guarantee that a site's future contents will continue to meet our high standards of quality and educational value. Be advised that students should be closely supervised whenever they access the Internet.

INDEX